Song
Book

# Play Guitar Today! Songbook

**Featuring 10 Rock & Pop Favorites!**

AF009459

Recording Credits:
Todd Greene & Rich Plath, Vocals
Scott Schroedl, Drums
Doug Boduch, Guitar
Tom McGirr, Bass
Jake Johnson, Engineer
Recorded at Sleepless Nights Recording Studios, Madison, WI

ISBN 0-634-00411-5

7777 W. BLUEMOUND RD. P.O. BOX 13819 MILWAUKEE, WI 53213



Visit Hal Leonard Online at
**www.halleonard.com**

# Introduction

Welcome to the *Guitar Songbook*. This book includes several well-known rock and pop favorites, and is intended for the beginner to intermediate player.

The ten songs in this book are carefully coordinated with the skills introduced throughout levels one and two of the method, *Play Guitar Today!* Refer to the right column in the table of contents below to know when you're ready to play each piece.

# Contents



# About the CD

A full-band recording of each song in the book is included on the CD, so you can hear how it sounds and play along when you're ready. Each example is preceded by one measure of "clicks" to indicate the tempo and meter. Pan right to hear the guitar part emphasized. Pan left to hear the accompaniment emphasized.

Before you begin, tune your guitar to the tuning notes on track 1.

# Song Structure

Most songs have different sections, that might be recognizable by any or all of the following:

- **Introduction** (or "Intro"): This is a short section at the beginning that "introduces" the song to the listeners.

- **Verses**: One of the main sections of the song—the part that includes most of the storyline—is the *verse*. There will usually be several verses, all with the same music but each with different lyrics.

- **Chorus**: Perhaps the most memorable section of the song is the *chorus*. Again, there might be several choruses, but each chorus will often have the same lyrics and music.

- **Bridge**: This section makes a transition from one part of a song to the next. For example, you may find a bridge between the chorus and next verse.

- **Solos**: Sometimes solos are played over the verse or chorus structure, but in some songs the solo section has its own structure. This is your time to shine!

- **Outro**: Similar to the "intro," this section brings the song to an end.

# Lyrics

All of the lyrics to all of the great songs in this book are included. They are shown above the staff in italics as a guide to help you keep your place in the music.

# Endings

Several of the songs have some new symbols that you must understand before playing. Each of these symbols represents a different type of ending.

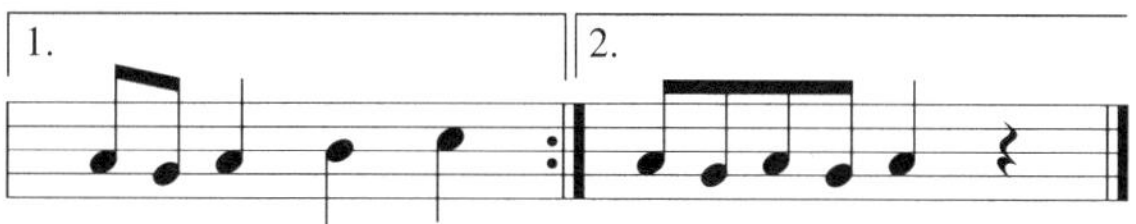

### First and Second Endings

Play the song through to the first ending, repeat back to the first repeat sign, or beginning of the song (whichever is the case). Play through the song again, but skip the first ending and play the second ending.

### D.S. al Coda

When you see these words, go back and repeat from this symbol: 𝄋

Play until you see the words "To Coda," then skip to the Coda, indicated by this symbol: 𝄌

Now just finish the song.

# Let It Be

Track 2

## Words and Music by John Lennon and Paul McCartney

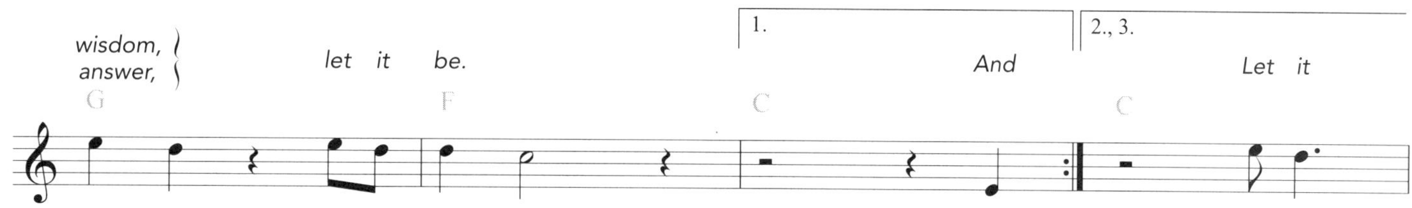

*Additional Lyrics*

2.  And when the broken hearted people
    Living in the world agree,
    There will be an answer, let it be.
    For tho' they may be parted
    There is still a chance that they will see,
    There will be an answer, let it be.

3.  And when the night is cloudy
    There is still a light that shines on me,
    Shine until tomorrow, let it be.
    I wake up to the sound of music
    Mother Mary comes to me,
    Speaking words of wisdom, let it be.

# Brown Eyed Girl

## Words and Music by Van Morrison



**Intro**

Moderately ♩ = 140

1. Hey, where did we go?          Days when the rains came,
2., 3. See Additional Lyrics



down in the hollow          playin' a new game,



laughing and a running, hey, hey,          skipping and a jumping.



In the misty morning fog with          our          hearts a thumpin' and you



my brown eyed girl.



You,          my          brown eyed          girl.

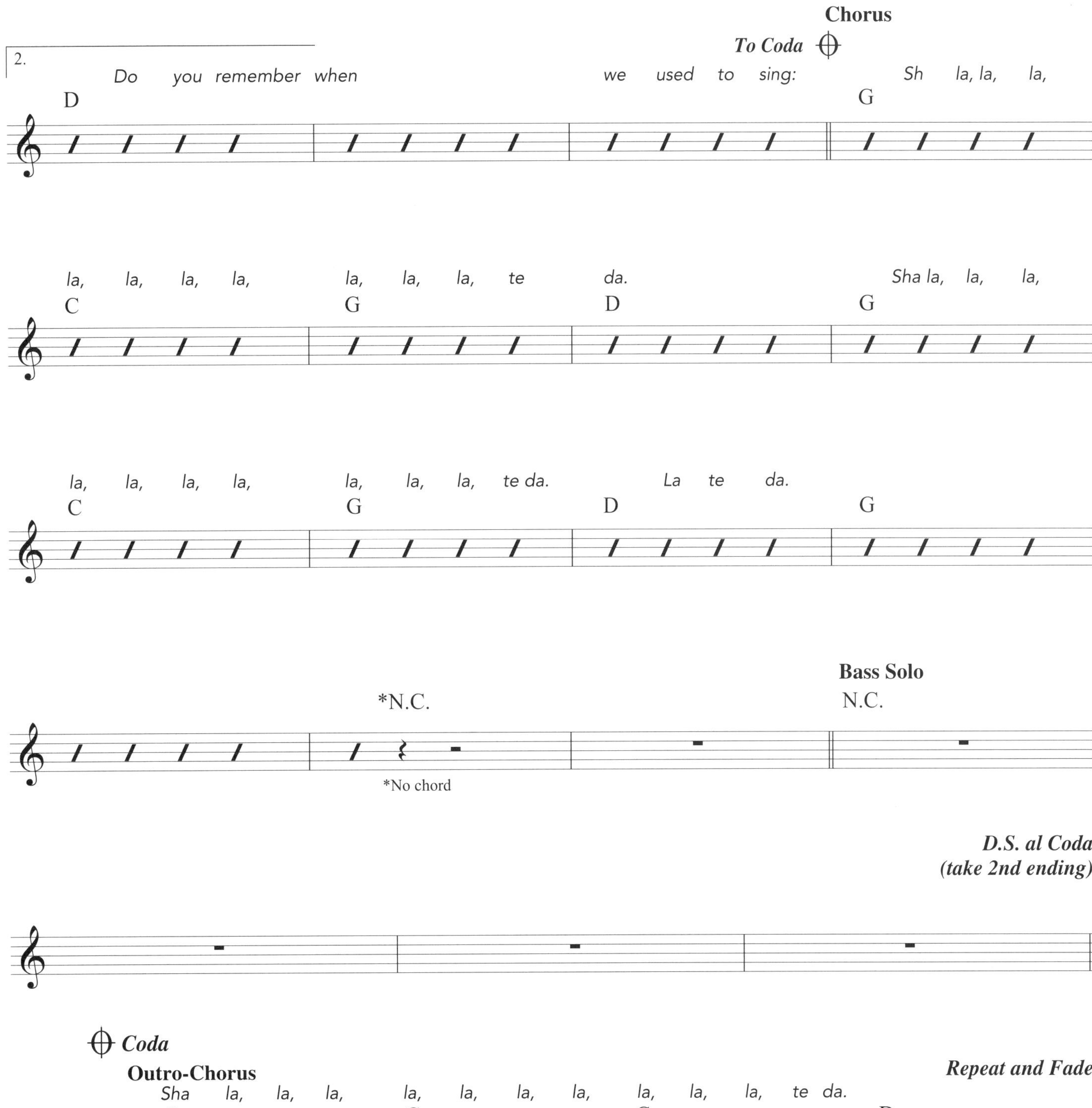


## Additional Lyrics

2. Whatever happened to Tuesday and so slow,
   Going down the old mine with a transistor radio?
   Standing in the sunlight laughing,
   Hiding behind a rainbow's wall,
   Slipping and a-sliding
   All along the waterfall
   With you, my brown eyed girl.
   You, my brown eyed girl.
   Do you remember when we used to sing;

3. So hard to find my way, now that I'm all on my own.
   I saw you just the other day, my, how you have grown.
   Cast my memory back there, Lord,
   Sometimes I'm overcome thinking 'bout it.
   Making love in the green grass
   Behind the stadium
   With you, my brown eyed girl.
   You, my brown eyed girl.
   Do you remember when we used to sing;

# Every Breath You Take

### Written and Composed by Sting

*Additional Lyrics*

2. Ev'ry single day, ev'ry word you say,
   Ev'ry game you play, ev'ry night you stay,
   I'll be watching you.

# Time Is on My Side



### Words and Music by Jerry Ragovoy



**Intro**
**Moderately**  ♩. = 74
(organ)

%: Chorus

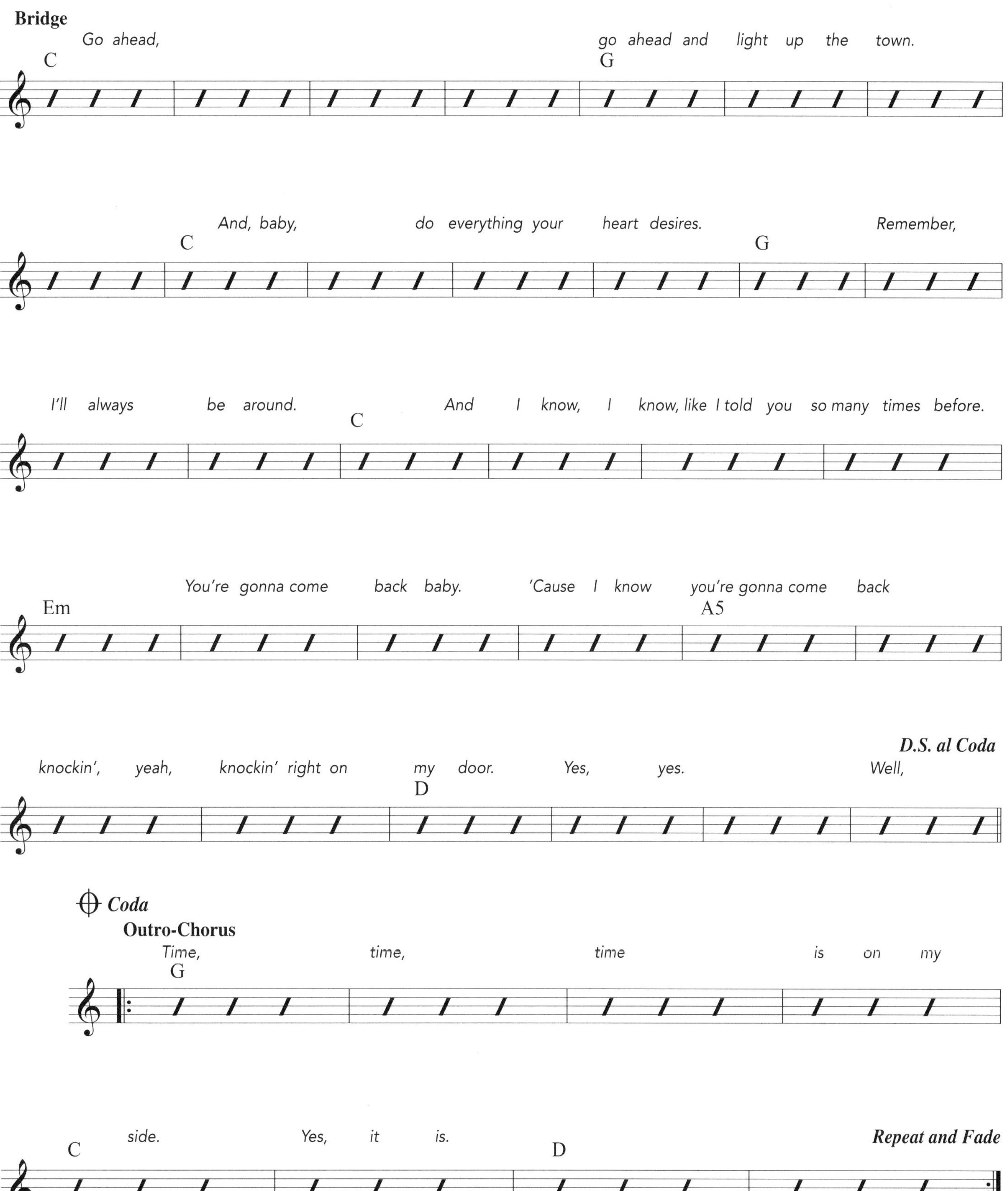


## Additional Lyrics

2. You're searchin' for good times, but just wait and see.
   You'll come runnin' back; I won't have to worry no more.
   You'll come runnin' back; spend the rest of my life with you, babe.
   You'll come runnin' back to me.

3. 'Cause I got the real love, the kind that you need.
   You'll come runnin' back; you said you would, baby.
   You'll come runnin' back; like I always said you would.
   You'll come runnin' back to me.

# Wild Thing

## Words and Music by Chip Taylor

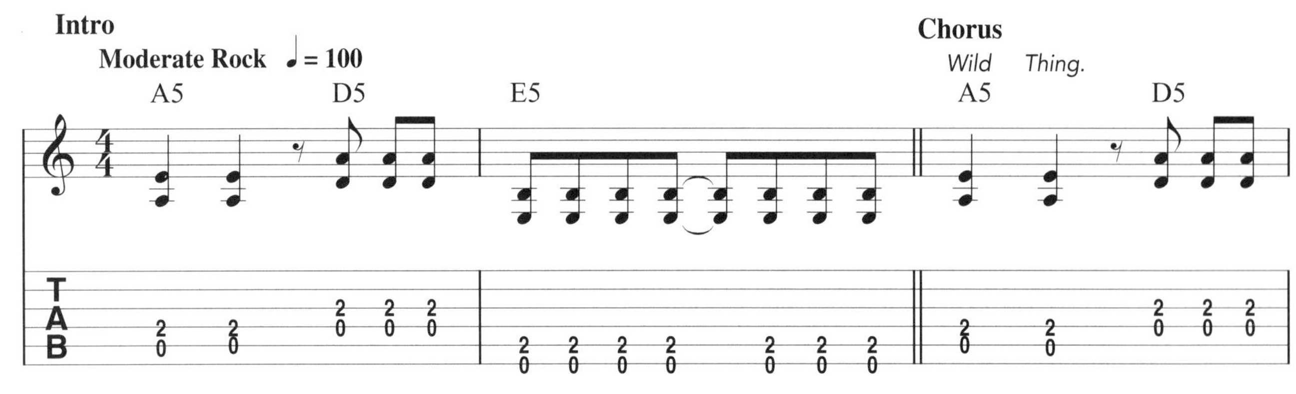

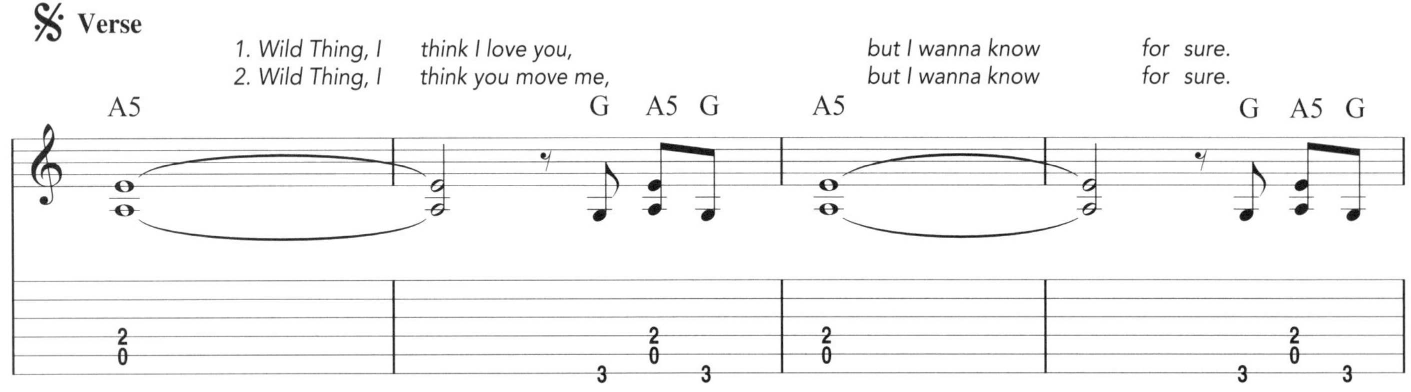


© 1965 (Renewed 1993) EMI BLACKWOOD MUSIC INC.
All Rights Reserved   International Copyright Secured   Used by Permission

Come on and
Come on and
hold
hold
me tight.
me tight.
I love you.
You move me.
A5
G  A5  G  A5

Interlude
A5  D5  E5  D5  A5  D5  E5  D5
To Coda

Chorus
Wild Thing,
you make my heart sing.
You make
A5  D5  E5  D5  A5  D5  E5  D5

everything groovy,
Wild Thing.
A5  D5  E5  D5  A5  D5  E5

Instrumental Solo
A5  D5  E5  D5  A5  D5  E5  D5

D.S. al Coda
A5   D5   E5   D5   A5   D5   E5   G A5 G
Coda
E5
Outro-Chorus
Wild   Thing,
A5   D5   E5   you make my D5
heart   sing.
A5   D5   E5   You make D5   everything A5   groovy, D5
Wild   Thing.
E5   D5   A5   D5   E5   D5   Wild   Thing. A5

(blank page to facilitate page turn)

# You Really Got Me

## Words and Music by Ray Davies

**Intro**
**Moderate Rock** ♩ = 130

Verse

1. Girl, you really got me goin'. You got me
2. See, don't ever set me free. I always

so I don't know what I'm doin'. Yeah, you really
wanna be by your side. Girl, you you really

got me now. You got me so I can't sleep at night.

Yeah, you really got me now. You got me so I don't know what I'm doin'. Oh,

Pre-Chorus
yeah, you really got me now. You got me so I can't sleep at night. You
Chorus
really got me. You
D5 C D5 C D5 C D5 C D5 C D5 C D5 C D5 C
really got me. You really got me.
To Coda
D5 C D5 C D5 C D5 C
1.
2.
Guitar Solo
N.C.
F5
D.S. al Coda
Coda
G5 F5 G5 F5 G5 F5 G5 F5
D5

# Oh, Pretty Woman

## Words and Music by Roy Orbison and Bill Dees

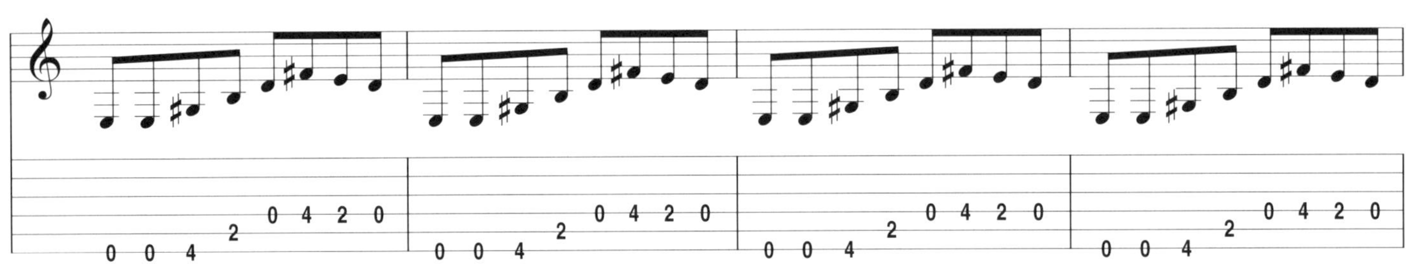

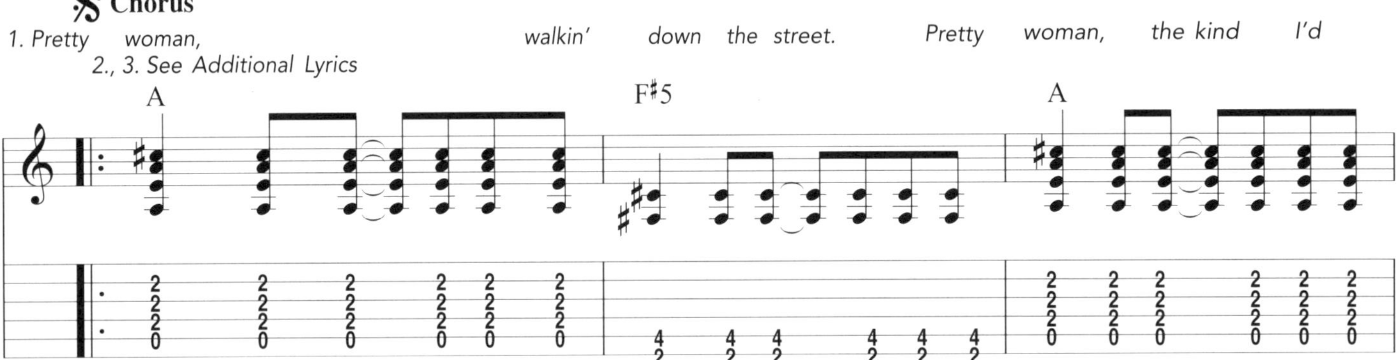


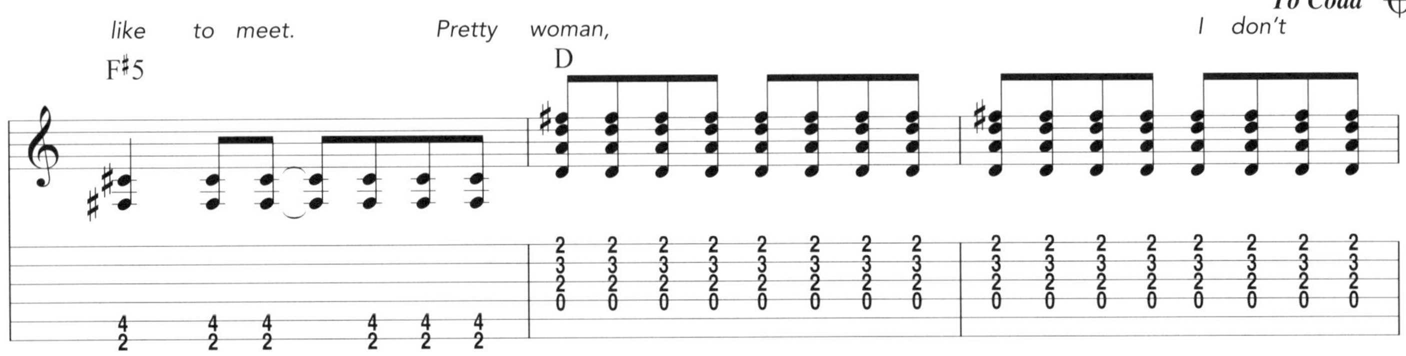


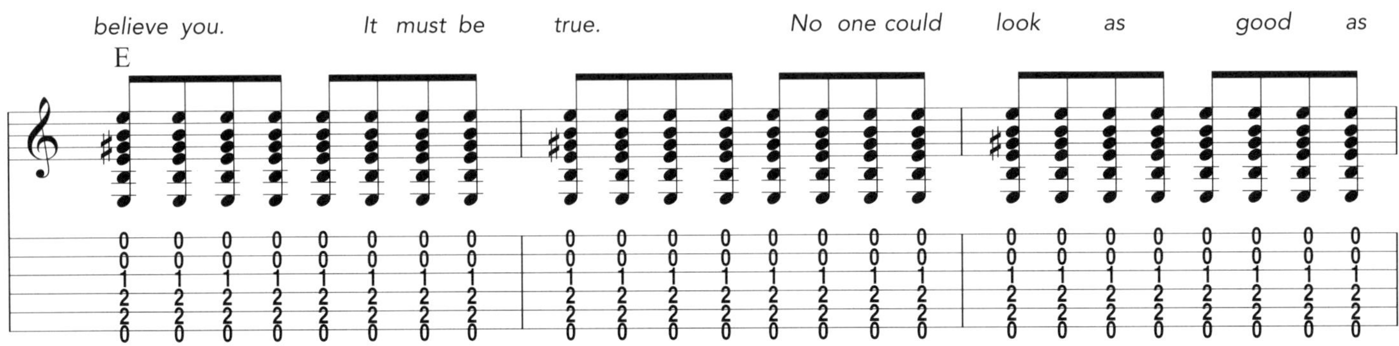

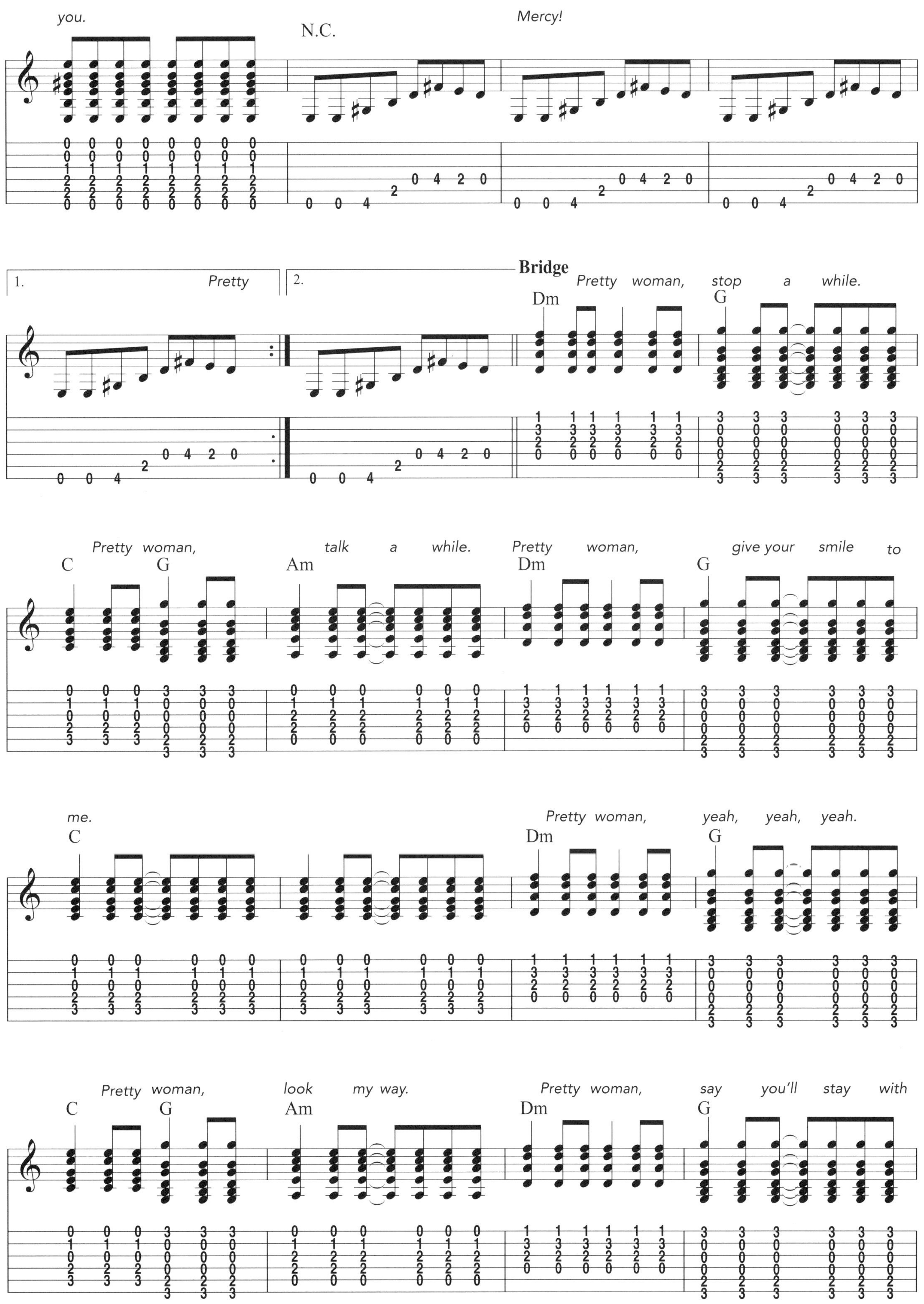

you.
N.C.
Mercy!
1.
Pretty
2.
Bridge
Pretty woman, stop a while.
Dm
G
Pretty woman,
C
G
talk a while.
Am
Pretty woman,
Dm
give your smile to
G
me.
C
Pretty woman, yeah, yeah, yeah.
Dm
G
Pretty woman,
C
G
look my way.
Am
Pretty woman,
Dm
say you'll stay with
G

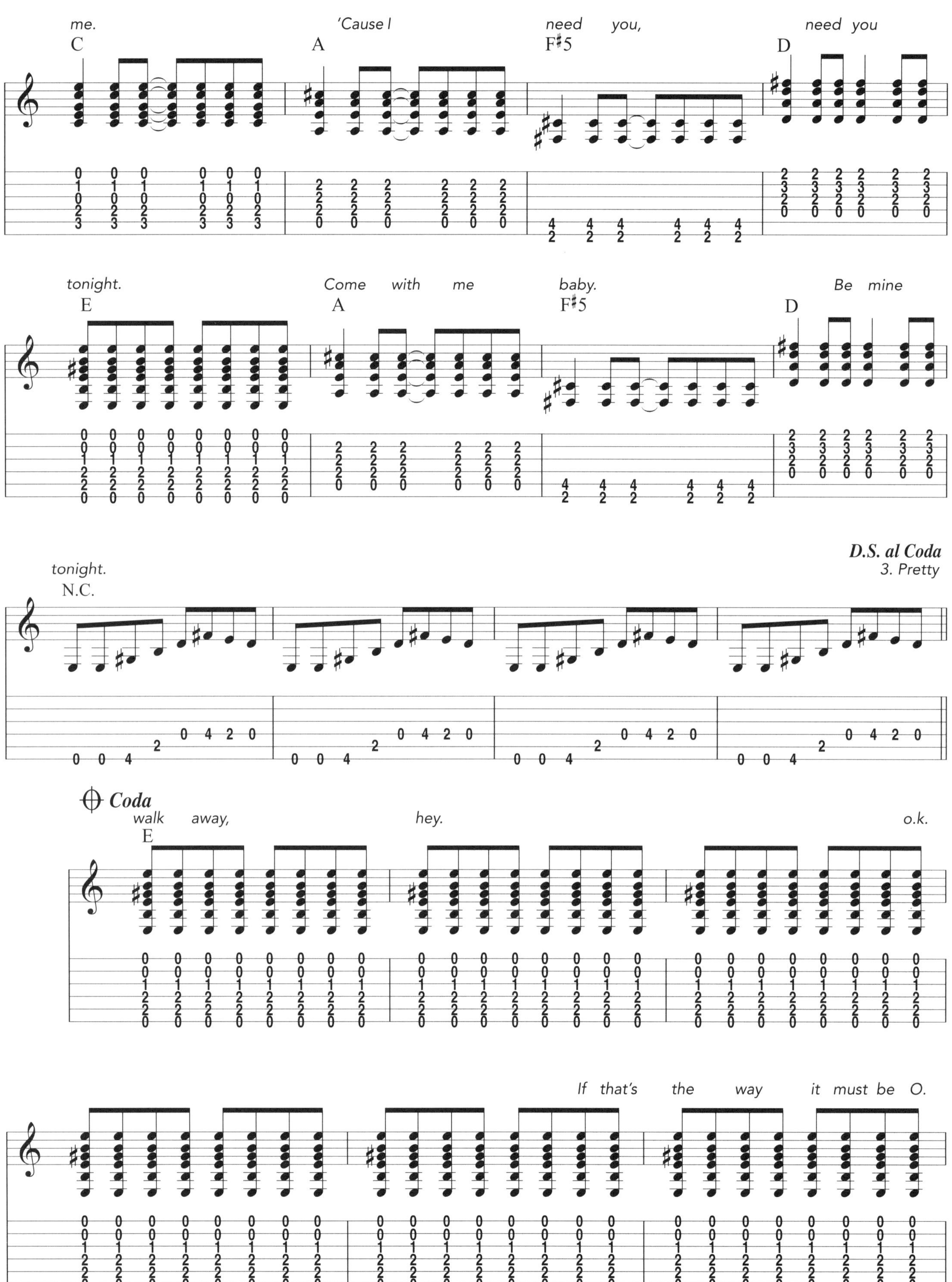

me.
C
'Cause I
A
need you,
F#5
need you
D
tonight.
E
Come with me
A
baby.
F#5
Be mine
D
tonight.
N.C.
D.S. al Coda
3. Pretty
Coda
walk away,
E
hey.
o.k.
If that's the way it must be O.

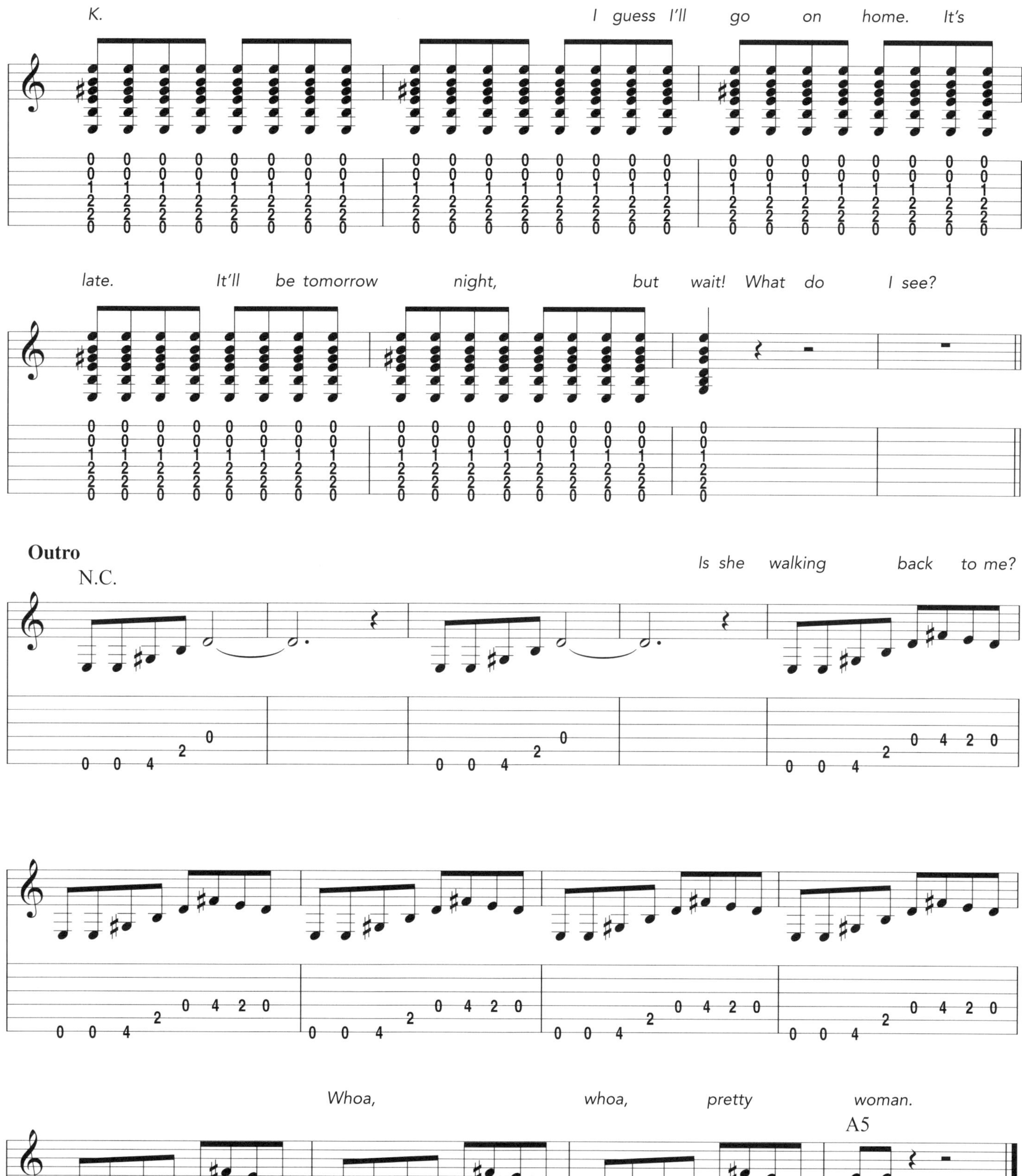


## Additional Lyrics

2. Pretty woman, won't you pardon me?
   Pretty woman, I couldn't help but see;
   Pretty woman, that you look lovely as can be.
   Are you lonely just like me?

3. Pretty woman, don't walk on by.
   Pretty woman, don't make me cry.
   Pretty woman, don't walk away, hey...

# American Pie



### Words and Music by Don McLean

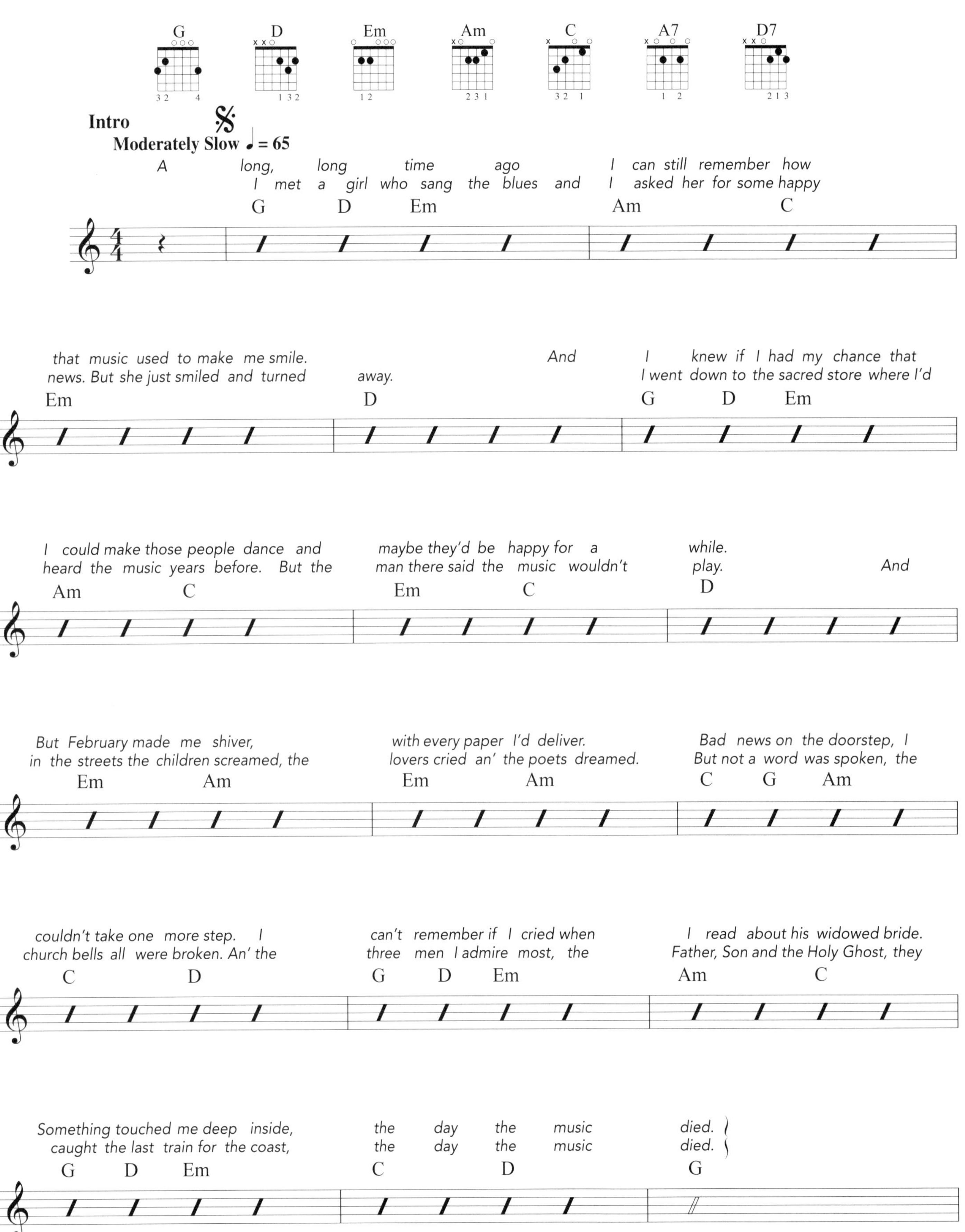

Chorus
Moderately ♩ = 102
So, bye, bye, Miss American Pie. Drove my
G C G D

Chevy to the levee, but the levee was dry. An' them good ol' boys were drinkin'
G C G D G C

whiskey an' rye, singin', "This'll be the day that I die,
G D Em A7

Faster ♩ = 142
To Coda
this'll be the day that I die."
Em D7

Verse
1. Did you write the book of love and do you have faith in
2., 3., 4. See Additional Lyrics
G Am C

God above, if the Bible tells you so?
Am Em D7

Now, do you believe in rock 'n' roll?" Can
G D Em

music save your mortal soul? An' can you teach me
Am C Em

how   to   dance   real   slow?   Well,   I
A7   D7
know   that   you're   in   love   with   him, 'cause I   saw   you   dancin'
Em   D   Em
in   the   gym.   You   both   kicked   off your   shoes.   Man,   I
D7   C   G   Am
dig   those   rhythm and blues.   I was a   lonely   teenage
C   D7   G   D
broncin'   buck   with   a   pink carnation   an'   a   pickup   truck.   But
Em   Am   C
I   knew   I   was out   of   luck,   the   day   the
G   D   Em   C
music   died.   I   started   singin',
D7   G   C   G   D
"Bye,   Bye,   Miss   American Pie.   Drove   my   Chevy   to the levee, but the
G   C   G   D   G   C

**Chorus**

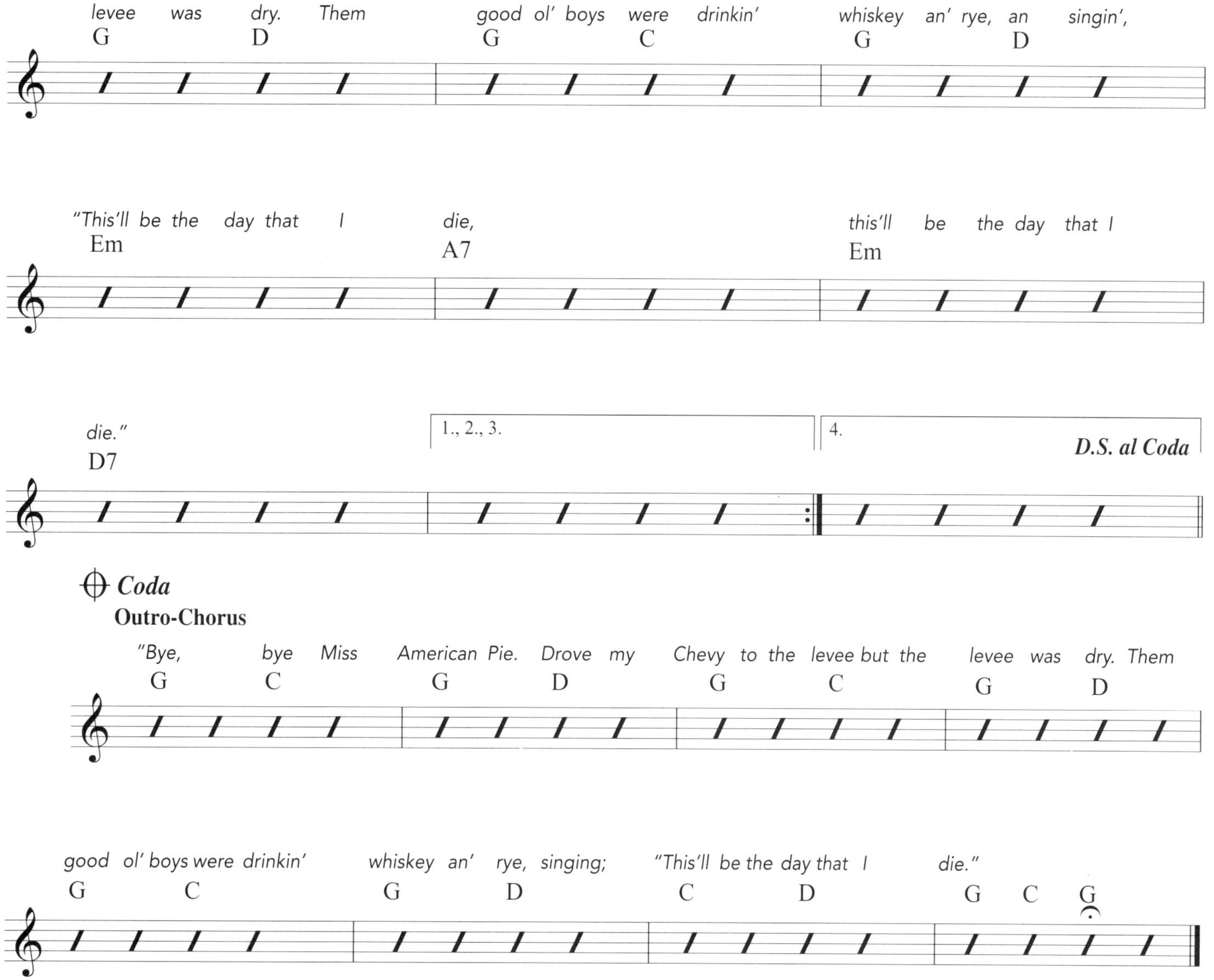


## Additional Lyrics

2. Now for ten years we've been on our own, an' moss grows fat on a
   rolling stone.
   But, that's not how it used to be.
   When the jester sang for the king an' queen in a coat he borrowed
   from James Dean.
   An' a voice that came from you and me.
   Oh, an' while the king was looking down, the jester stole his thorny
   crown.
   The courtroom was adjourned; no verdict was returned.
   And while Lenin read a book on Marx, a quartet practiced in the park.
   And we sang dirges in the dark, the day the music died. We started
   singin'…

3. Helter, skelter in the summer swelter.
   The birds flew off for the fallout shelter, eight miles high an' fallin' fast.
   It landed foul out on the grass.
   The players tried for a forward pass, with the jester on the sidelines in a
   cast.
   Now, the halftime air was sweet perfume, while the sergeants played a
   marchin' tune.
   We all got up to dance, oh, but we never got the chance.
   'Cause the players tried to take the field, the marching band refused to
   yield.
   Do you recall what was revealed the day the music died? We started
   singin'…

4. Oh, an' there we were all in one place;
   A generation lost in space, with no time left to start again.
   So, come on, Jack be nimble, Jack be quick,
   Jack Flash sat on a candle stick, 'cause fire is the devil's only friend.
   Oh, and as I watched him on the stage my hands were clenched in fists
   of rage.
   No angel born in Hell could break that Satan's spell.
   And as the flames climbed high into the night to light the sacrificial rite,
   I saw Satan laughing with delight, the day the music died? He was
   singing'…

# Born to Be Wild

Track 10

## Words and Music by Mars Bonfire

**Intro**

Heavy Rock ♩ = 148

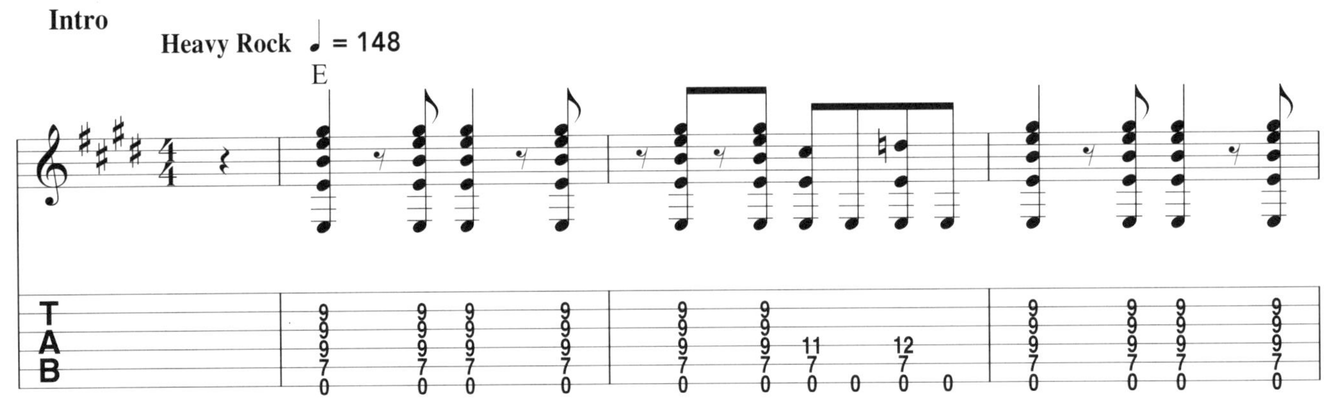

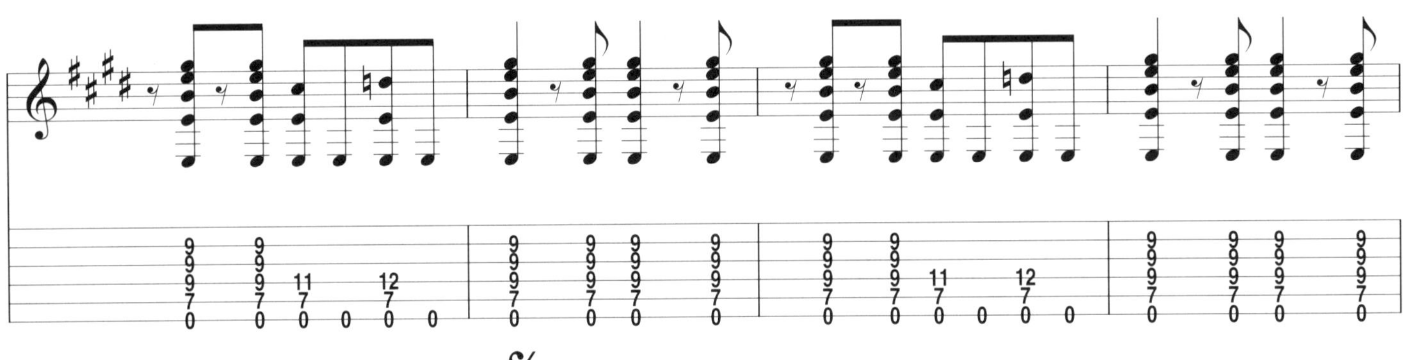

**𝄋 Verse**

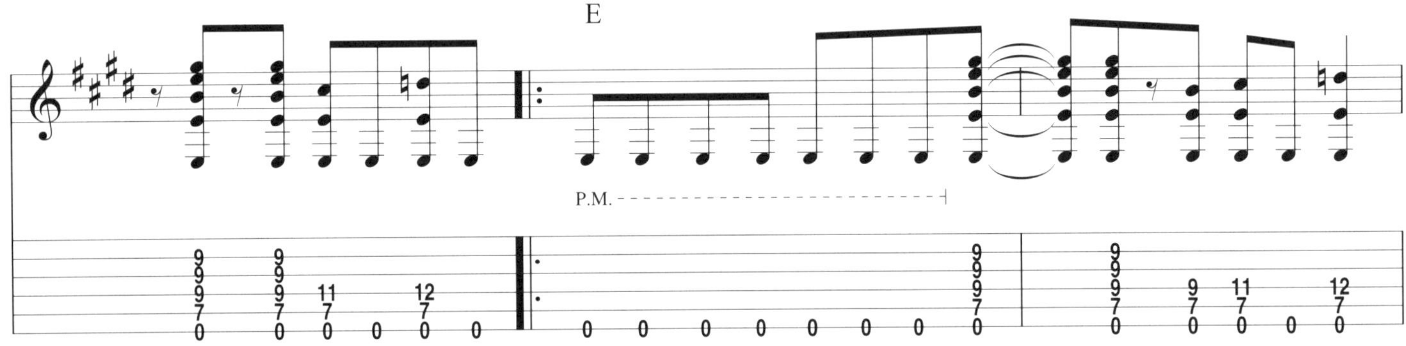



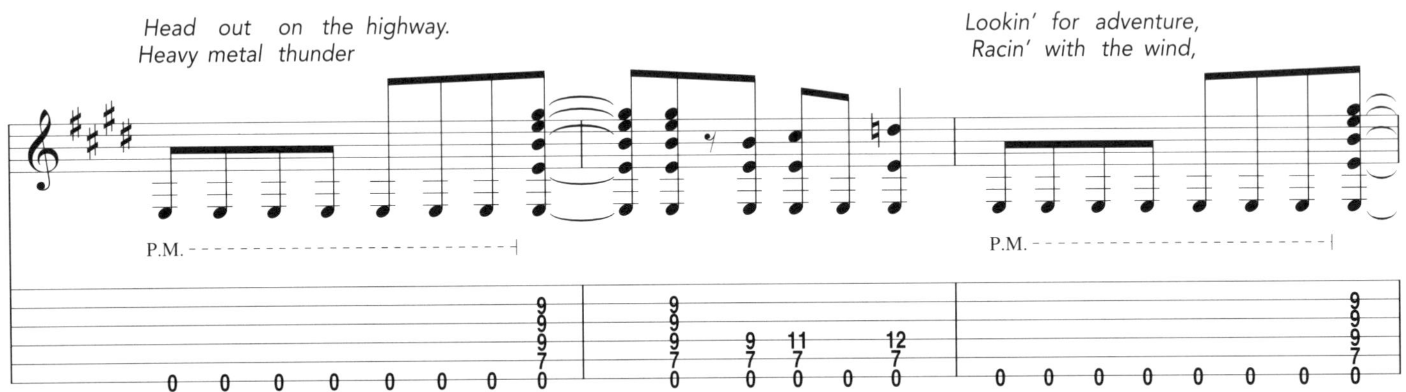

and whatever comes our way.
and the feelin' that I'm under.
E
P.M.
Yeah, darlin' gonna make it happen.
G        A        E
Take the world in a
G        A
full
love embrace.
E
Fire all of your guns at once and
G        A        E
explode into
G        A
full
1.
space.
E
2.
space. Like a true nature's child we were
E
born, born to be wild.
G
We can climb so high.
A
I never wanna
G

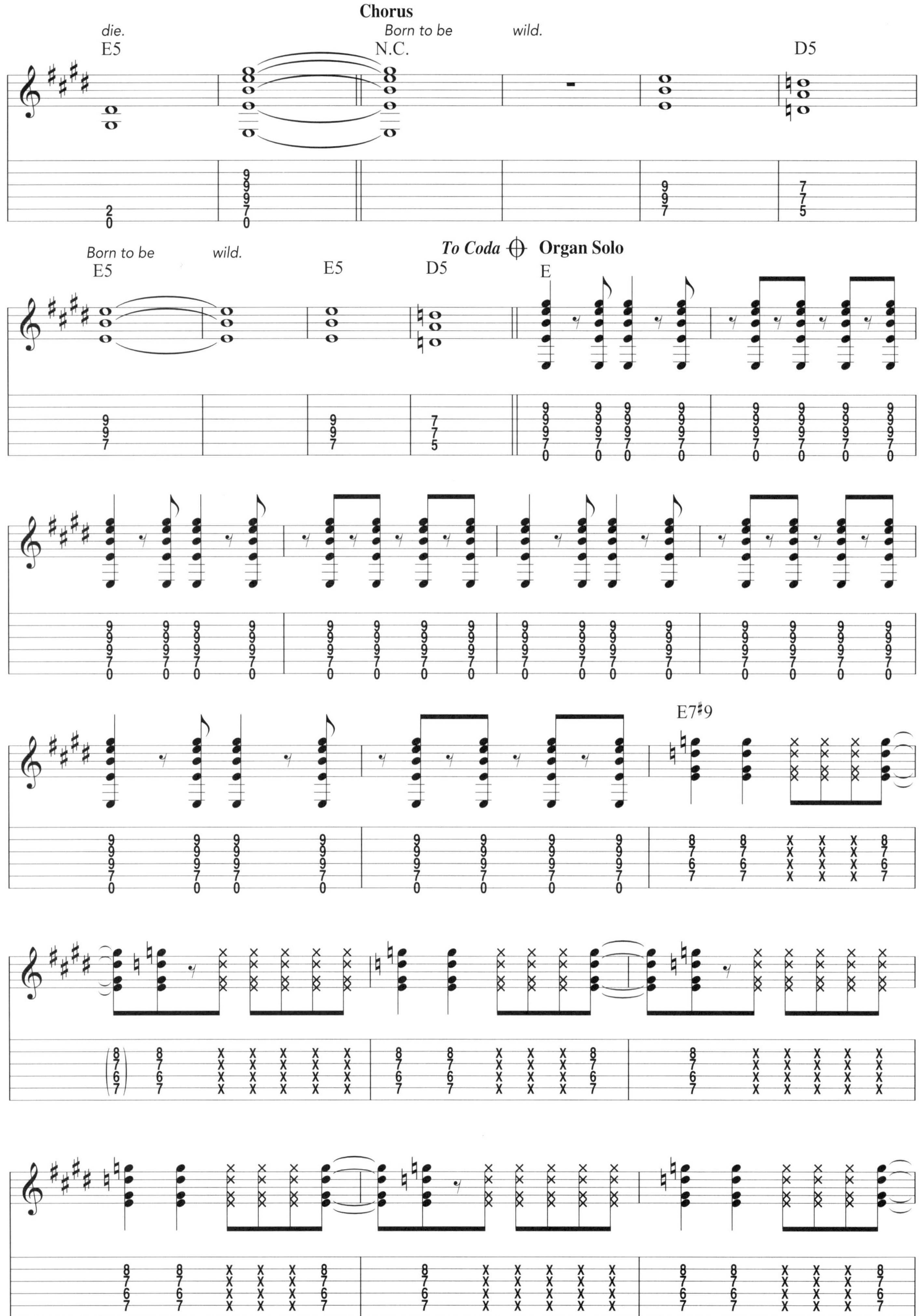

Chorus
die.
Born to be wild.
E5
N.C.
D5
Born to be wild.
E5
E5
D5
To Coda
Organ Solo
E
E7#9
28

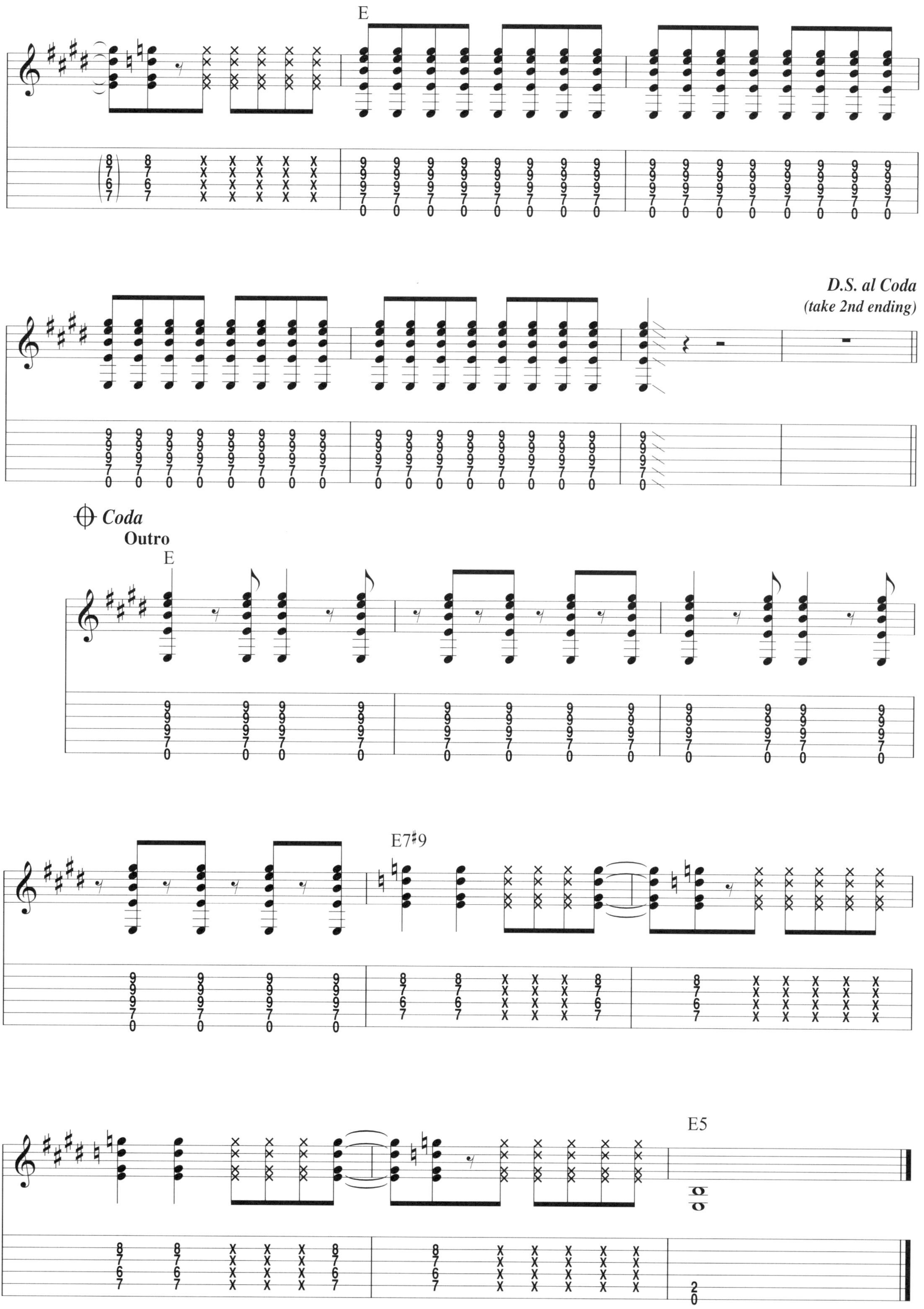

# I Shot the Sheriff



## Words and Music by Bob Marley

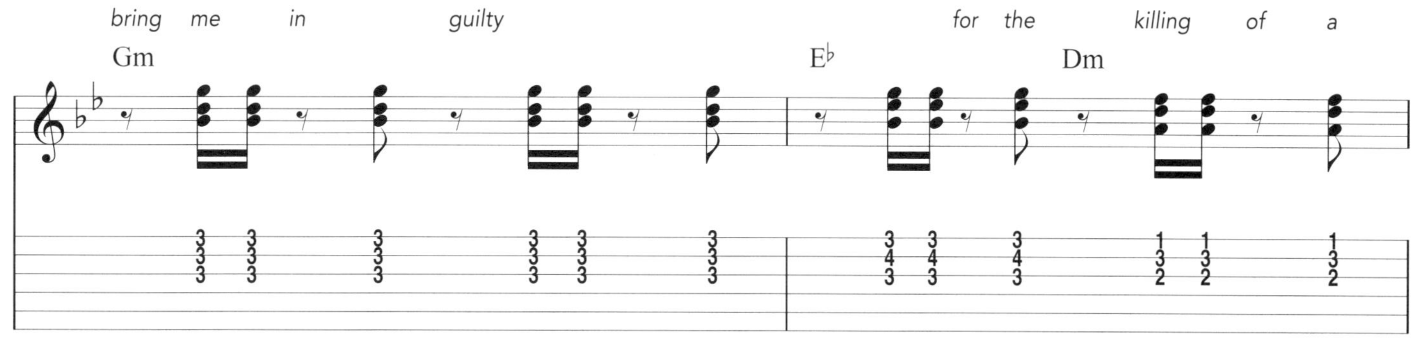


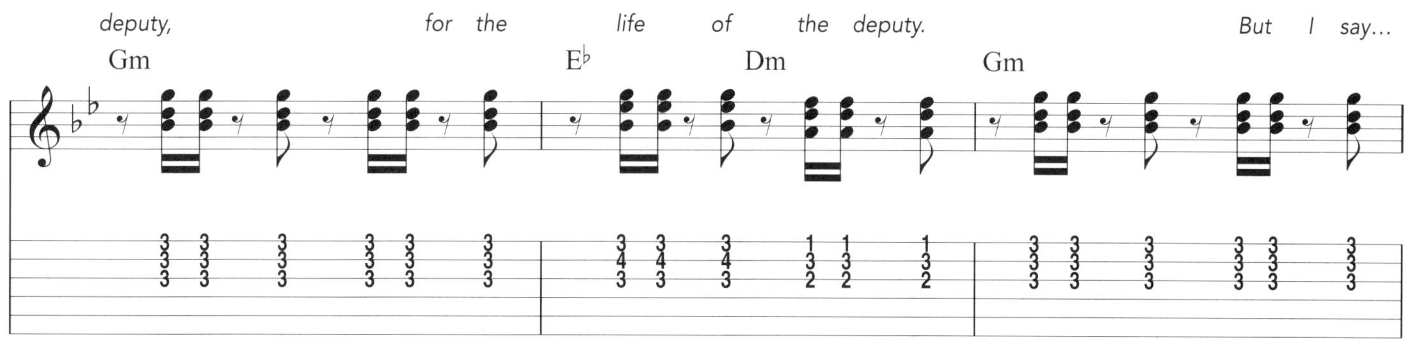

## Additional Lyrics

2. Sheriff John Brown always hated me;
   For what I did I don't know.
   And every time I try to plant that little seed,
   He said, "Kill it before it grows,"
   "Kill it before it grows."

3. Freedom came my way one fine day,
   So I headed straight out of town.
   All of a sudden, I see Sheriff John Brown
   Aimin' to shoot me down,
   So I shot I shot him down.

4. Reflexes got the better of me,
   What will be will be.
   Everytime the bucket goes to the well,
   One day the bottom will drop out
   One day the bottom will drop out.

# Play Guitar Today!